M²/4   11A

The Bouncy Moose

and other cartoons

By Simon French

The Big Eyes Press
Devon, England

Published by The Big Eyes Press

Devon, England

Printed and bound in England

ISBN: 978-0-9559020-0-0

About The Author

Born in 1979 with his mother at his side, Simon French was immediately picked out by the midwife as a child with enormous artistic potential. This became apparent as she witnessed him arranging his unsevered umbilical cord into the shape of a heart and then laying it beside the face of his exhausted mother.

This book is the first collection of Simon's cartoons to be published. These have been drawn, not onto paper, but directly into the computer world of electricity and numbers. Simon uses a mouse to draw his cartoons (make of that what you will).

The simplicity of getting from A to B when you have nothing to worry about and no one to bother you.

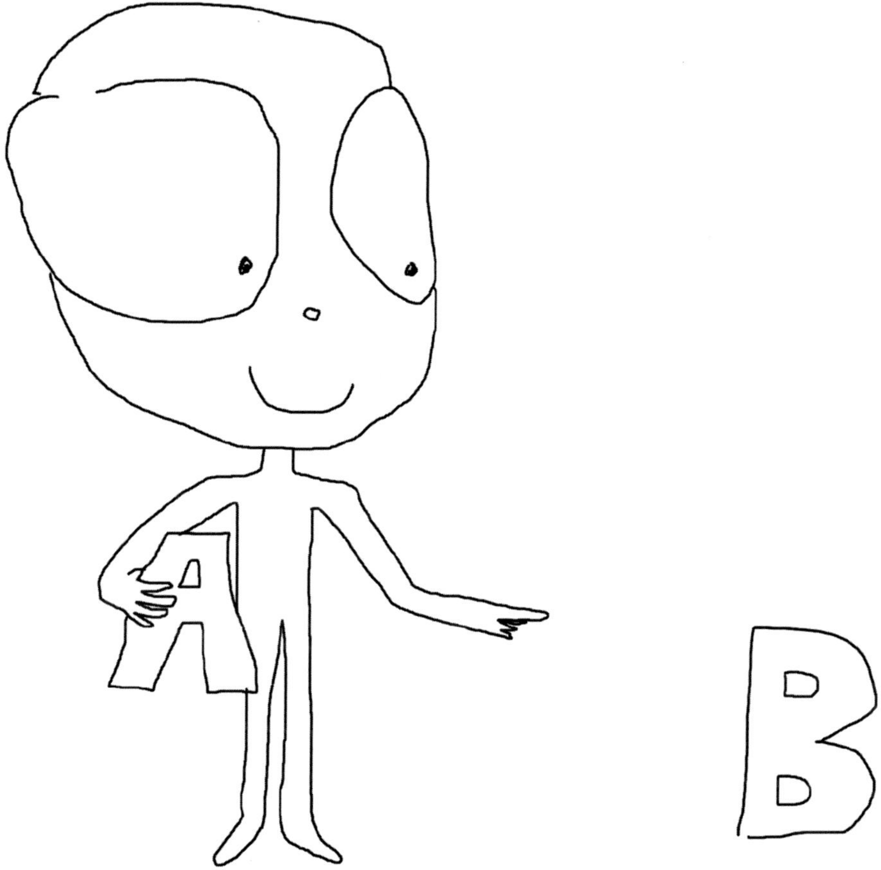
A
B

A father tries to explain the shortcomings of Communism to his son, using only a rubber ball and a piece of string. The son interrupts, but only to ask for the string.

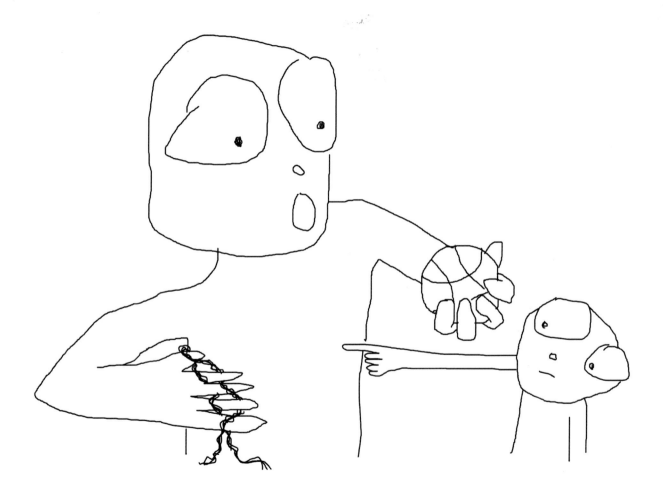

Woman running from her own vanity towards the house of simple pleasures.

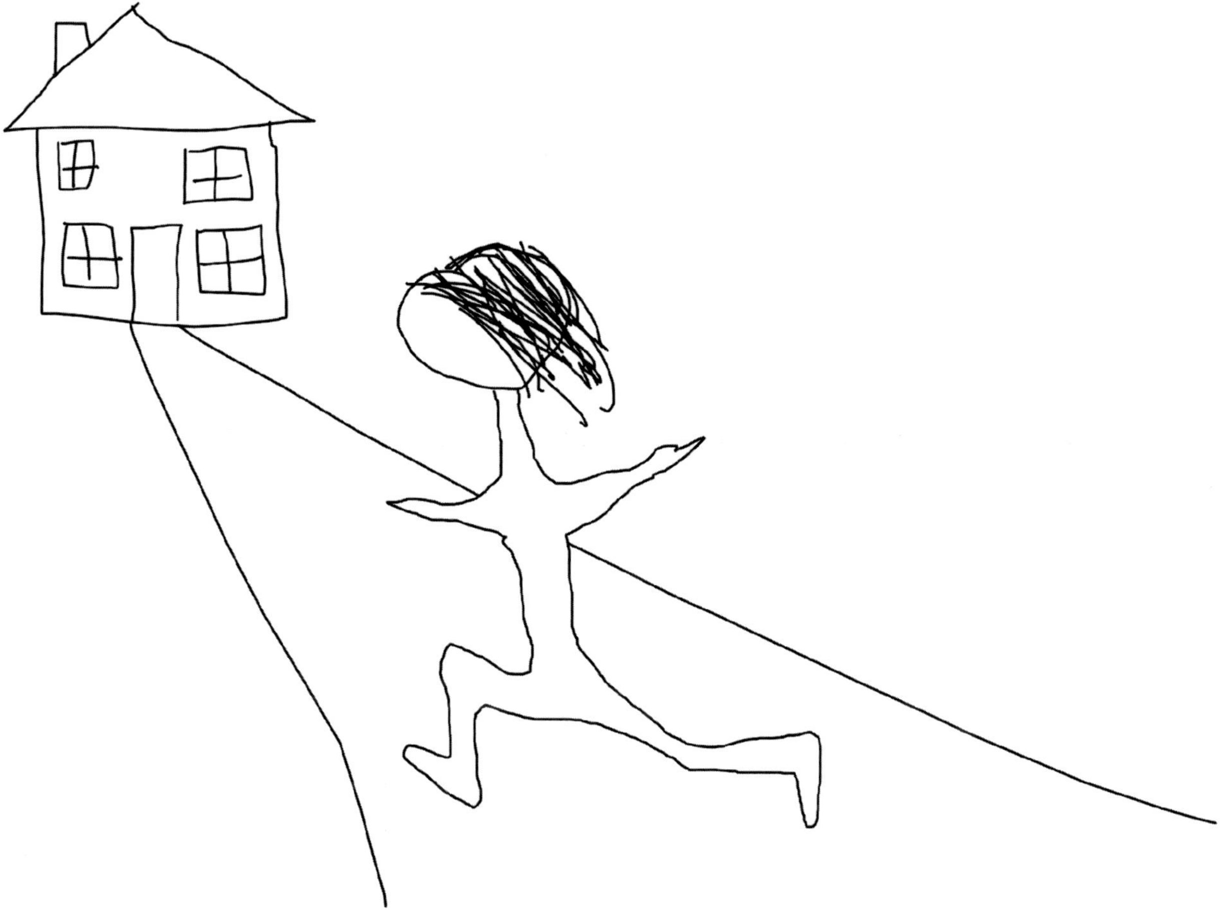

Today he is King! The wheelie confirms his standing: he is the coolest boy in the playground.

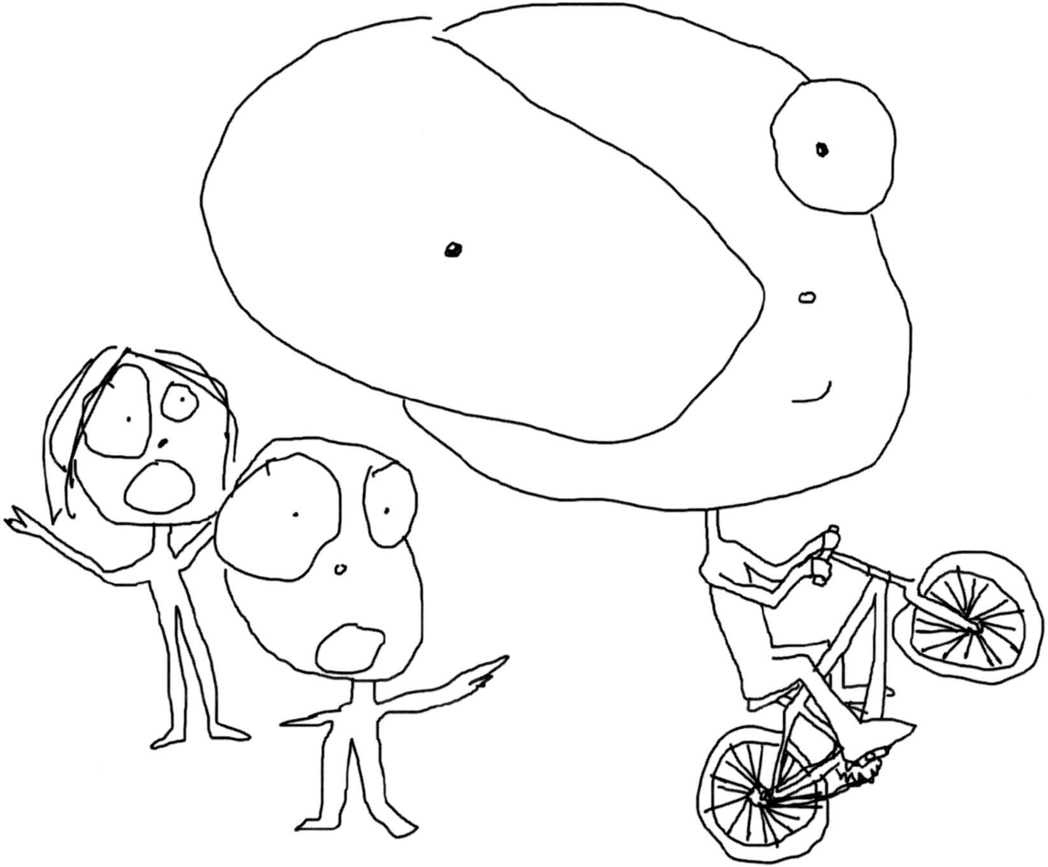

A young couple stroll through a wild-flower meadow; the dappled light plays across the tips of the long grass, as it bends and leans in the breeze. The pair seem to be at one with each other and with the landscape in which they are immersed, yet neither one gives a moment's thought to the beauty of their surroundings: the woman is thinking about a lovely hat she saw in the sales, and the man, pornography.

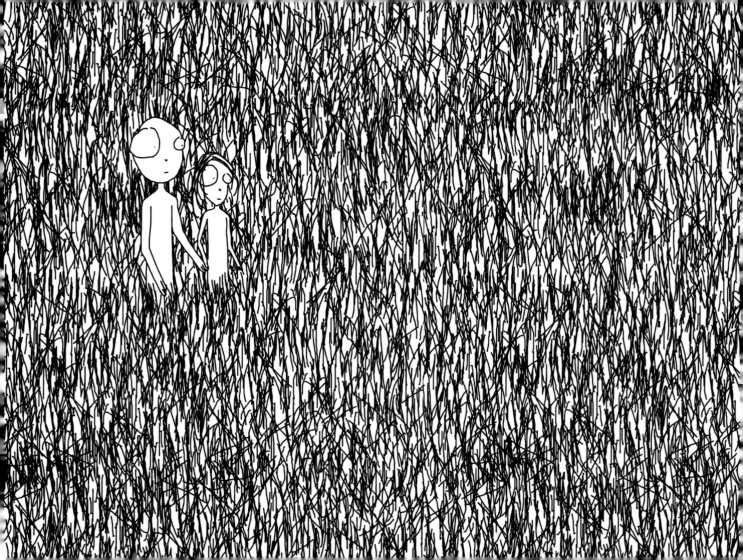

Even the ones in the distance have their own thoughts.

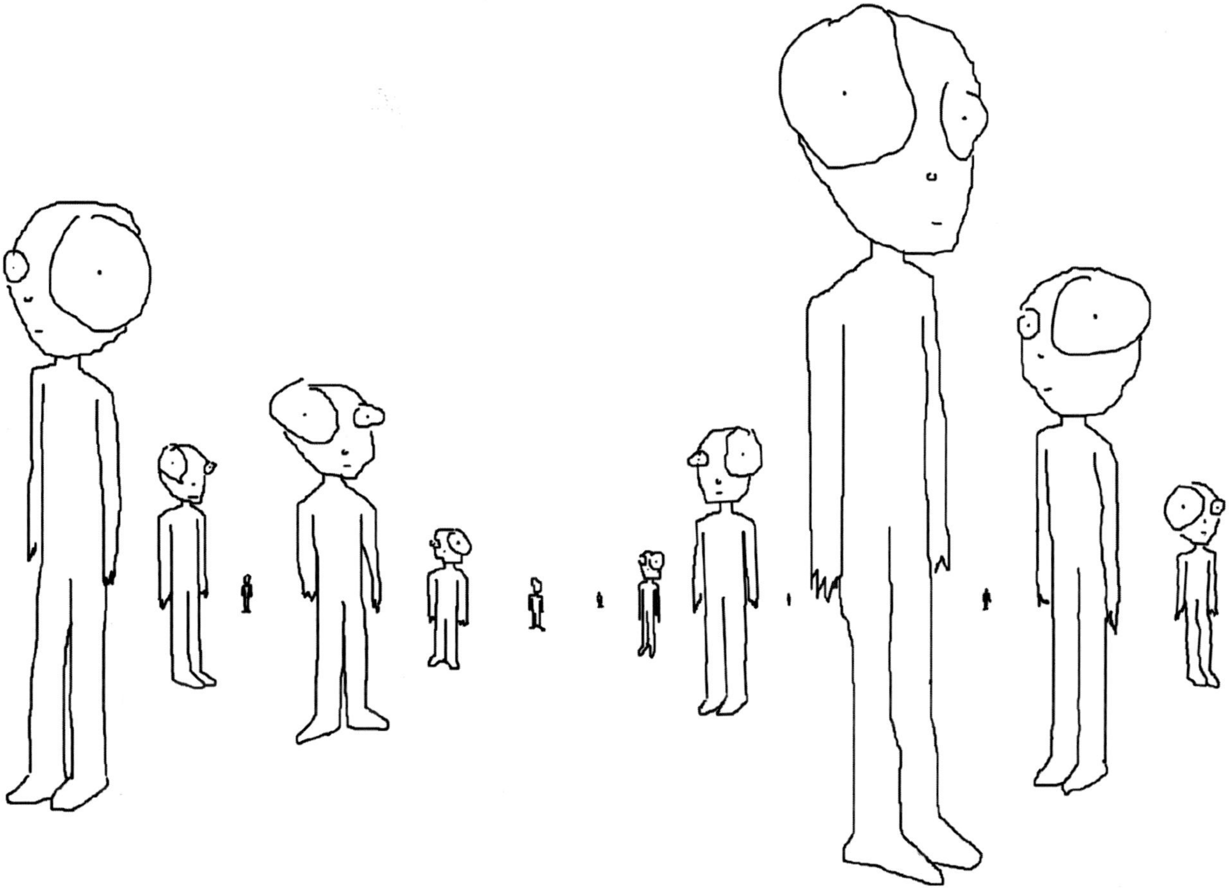

Two men stand and stare at each other in disbelief; each man is repulsed by the other, considering him to be a 'freak of nature'. To the side stands a tiny, asexual, human test-drone, searching for an identity.

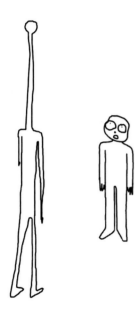

A young lady applies just the right amount of make-up before a night out. She hopes that tonight she will find a husband.

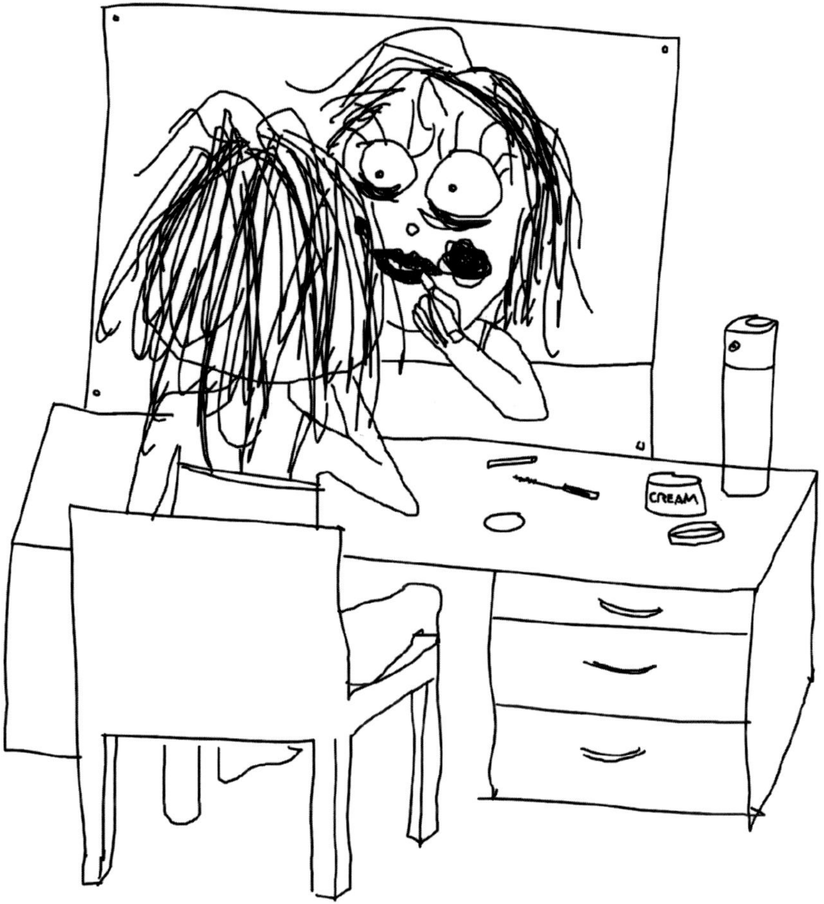
CREAM

In between each can, he remembered the potential he had shown in school. But the cans keep coming.

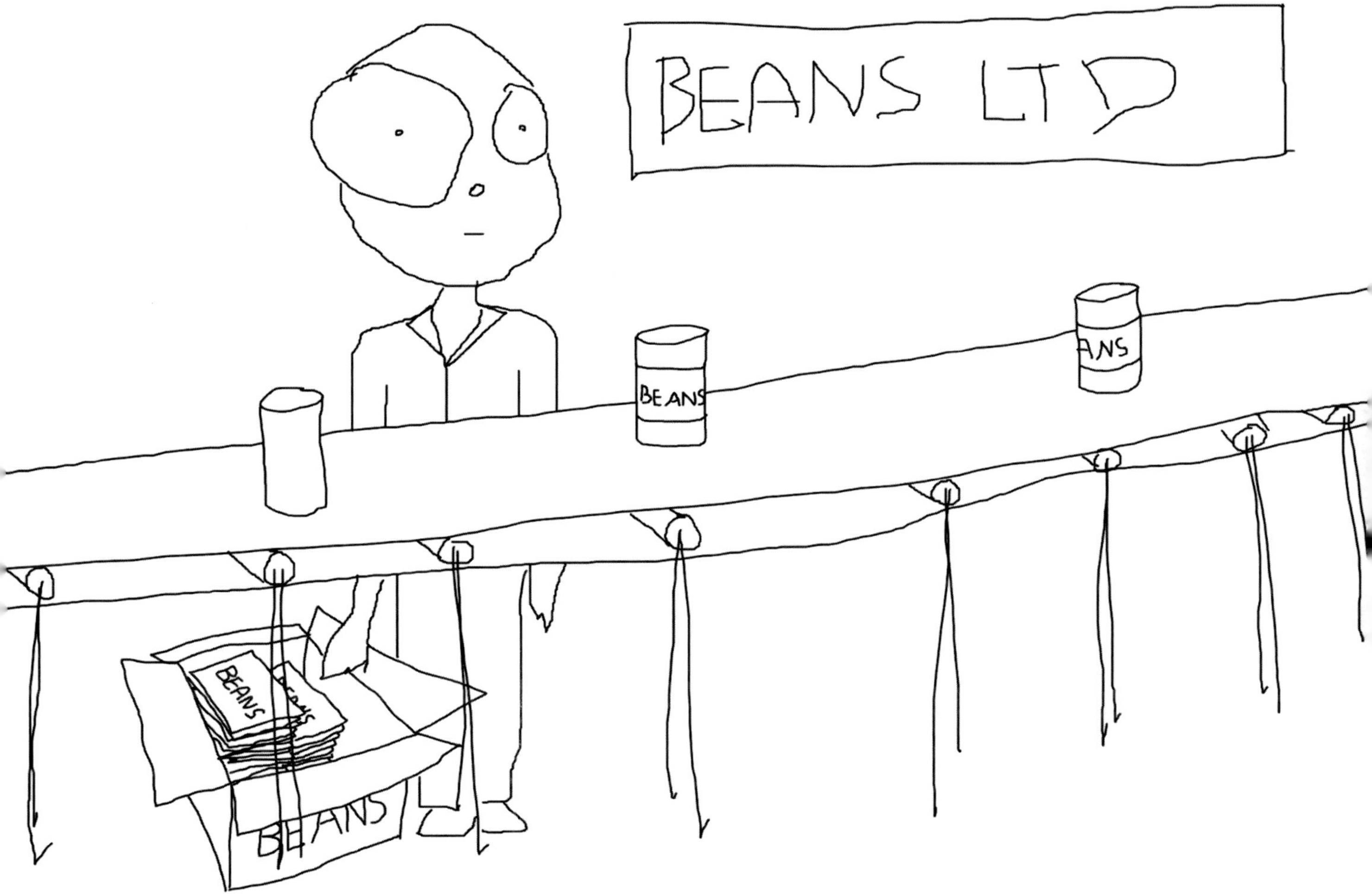
BEANS LTD
BEANS
ANS
BEANS
BEANS

This man is trapped on a stone slab by the weight of his own head.

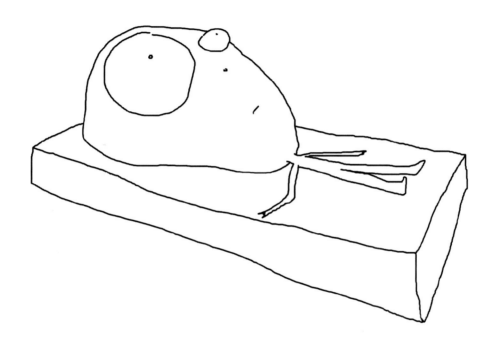

The Grandson is disappointed when his Grandfather will not wake up to look at his model of a German Stuka from the Second World War. The Grandson has a saucepan on his head. The saucepan would not be necessary against a plane the size of the model, yet he understands that in the war the real Stuka was a deadly enemy. If he explains this to his Grandfather when he wakes up, it may help them both. The Grandfather may finally talk about his experiences of the war, helping him come to terms with the defining chapter of his life, while the Grandson could better understand the extent of the conflict, and the effect it had on a generation.

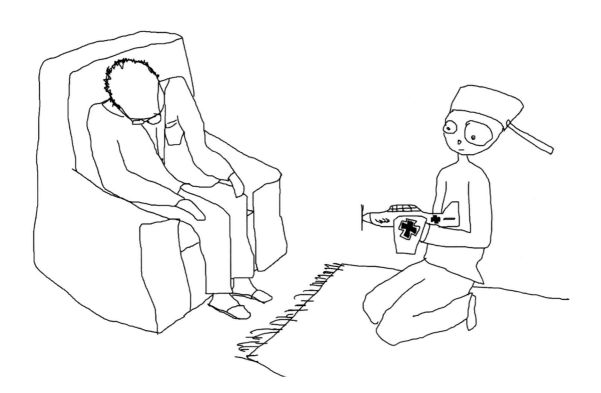

A ruthless collector tricks an unsuspecting child out of the precious pyramid shape; the cube is of no value.

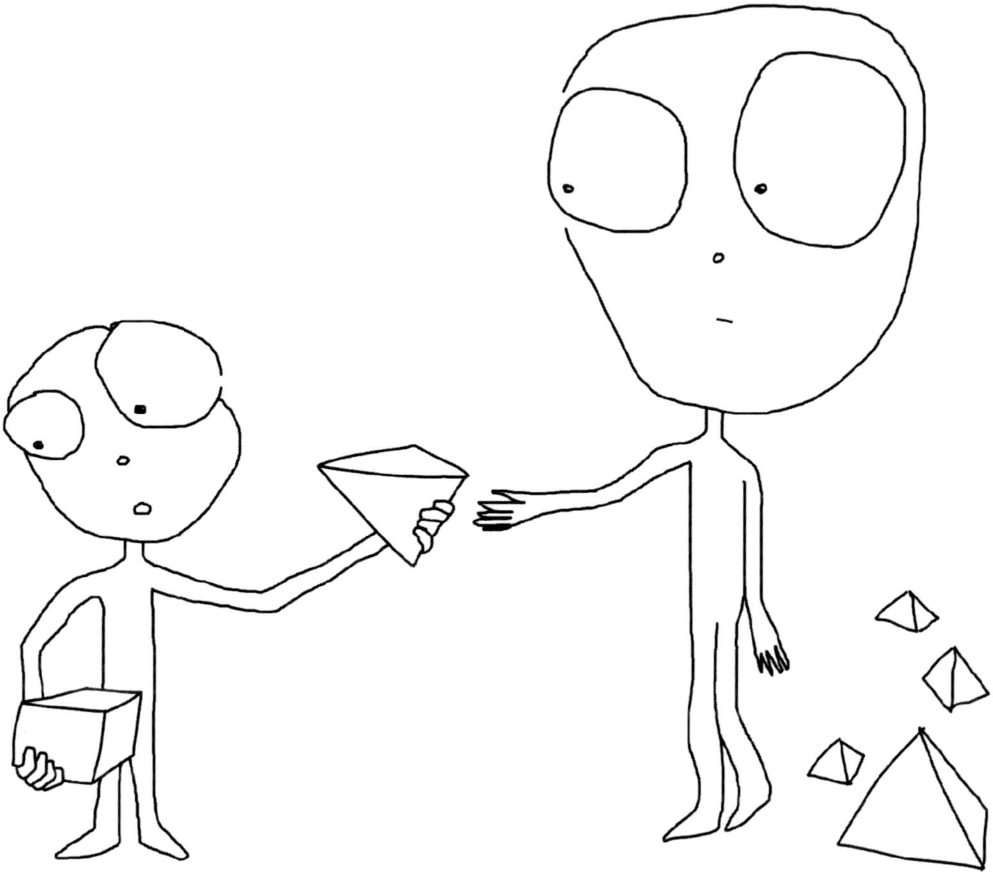

The man who planted management consultants.

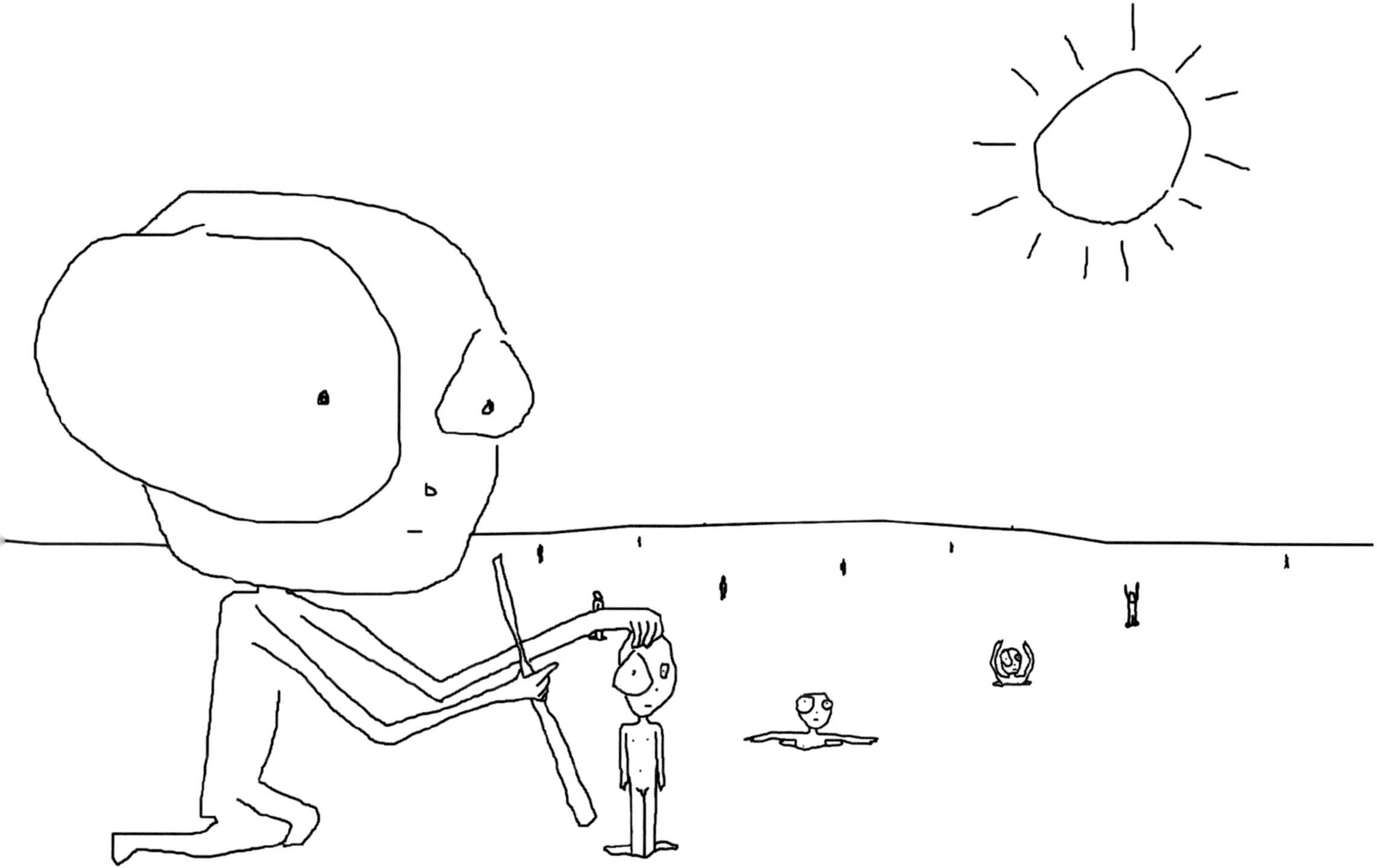

He is everything a woman wants in a man: strong of chin, broad of shoulders, barrelled of chest, wise of eyes, honest of elbow, staunch of feet, with a dynamic finger-pointing action and a non-conformist stance.

A small man teaching a large man the importance of diversity in modern culture.

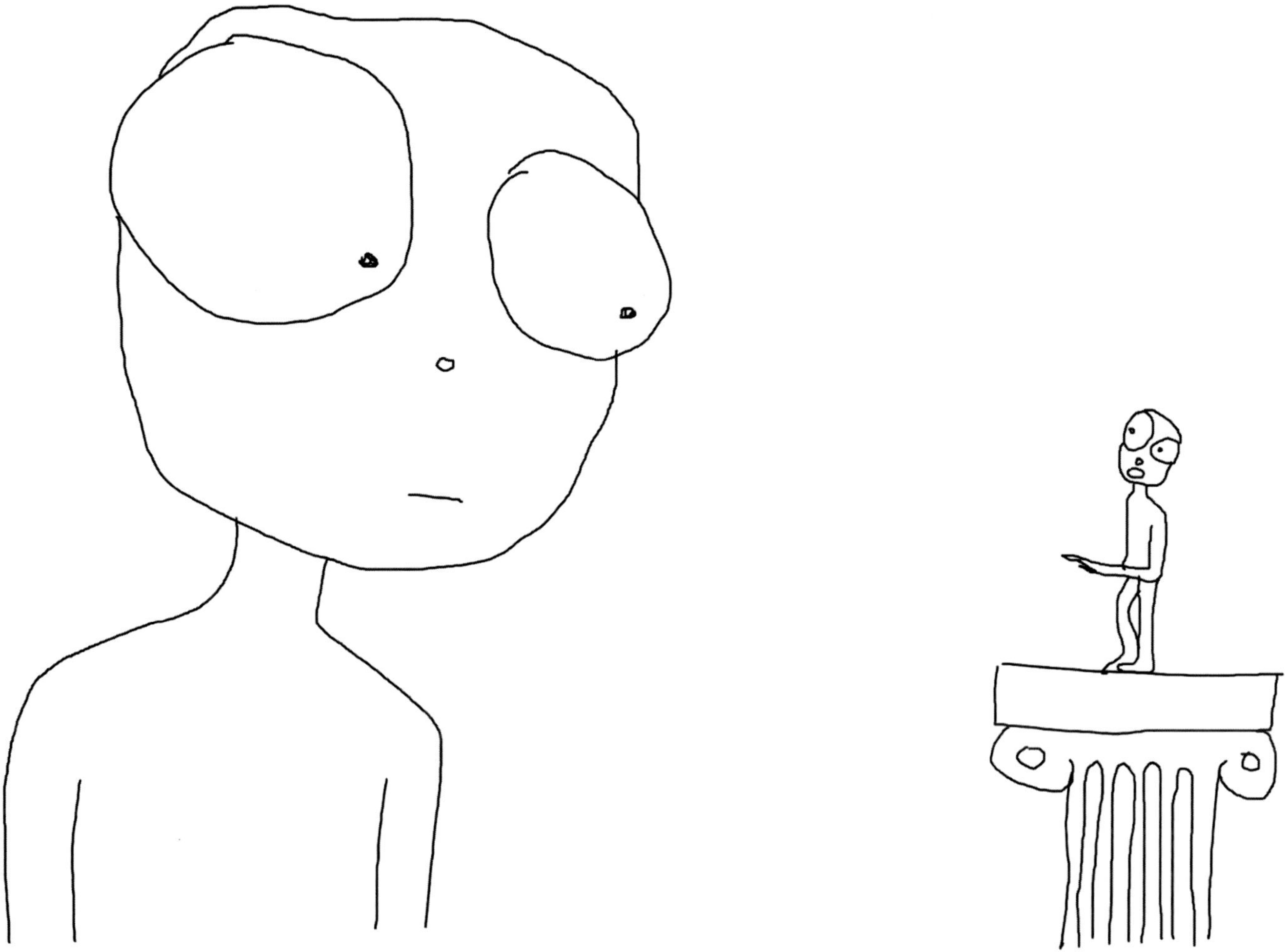

A fisherman describes 'The one that got away' to his nephew. The nephew is unimpressed. He is holding one that didn't get away. The fish also happens to be bigger than his uncle's imaginary, arm-span-restricted dream-fish.

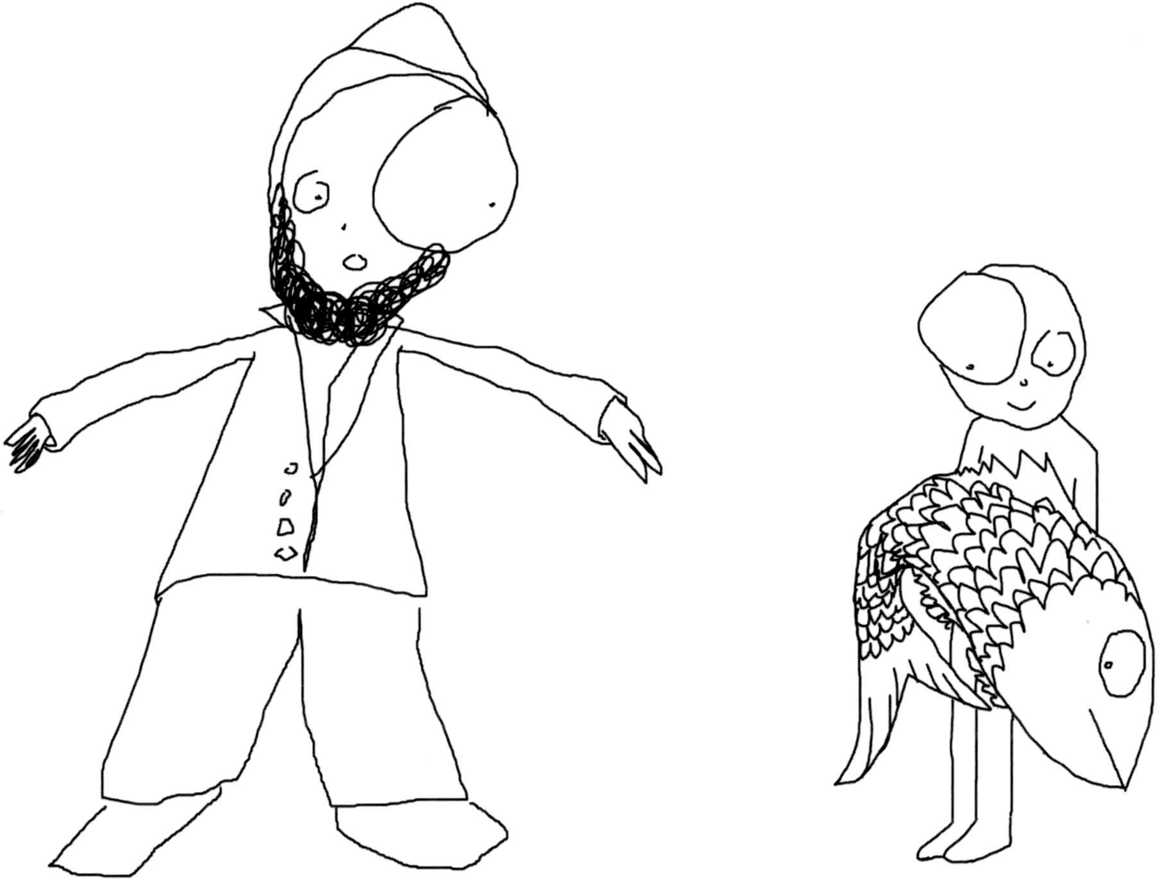

A man is standing on the summit of a mountain. He is all alone, with no one to talk to, no one to share the experience, and no one to hold; finally he is happy.

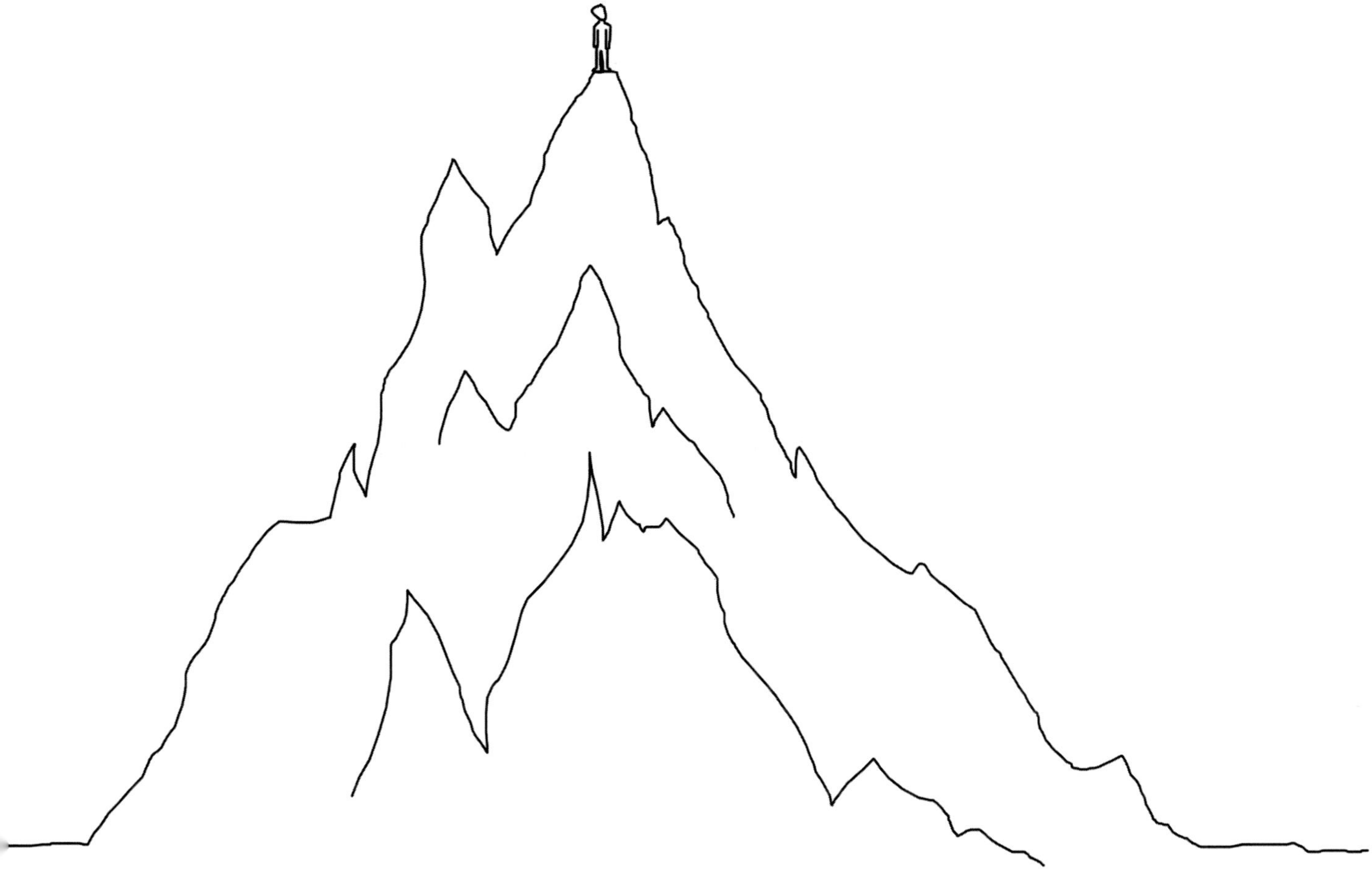

A toddler comes face to face with the bouncy moose. This is a meeting that he will remember for the rest of his life, a meeting that will help to define many of his future relationships.

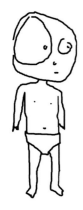

A gang of kids is waiting for a fight outside the school gates. Some of them don't want the fight to happen.

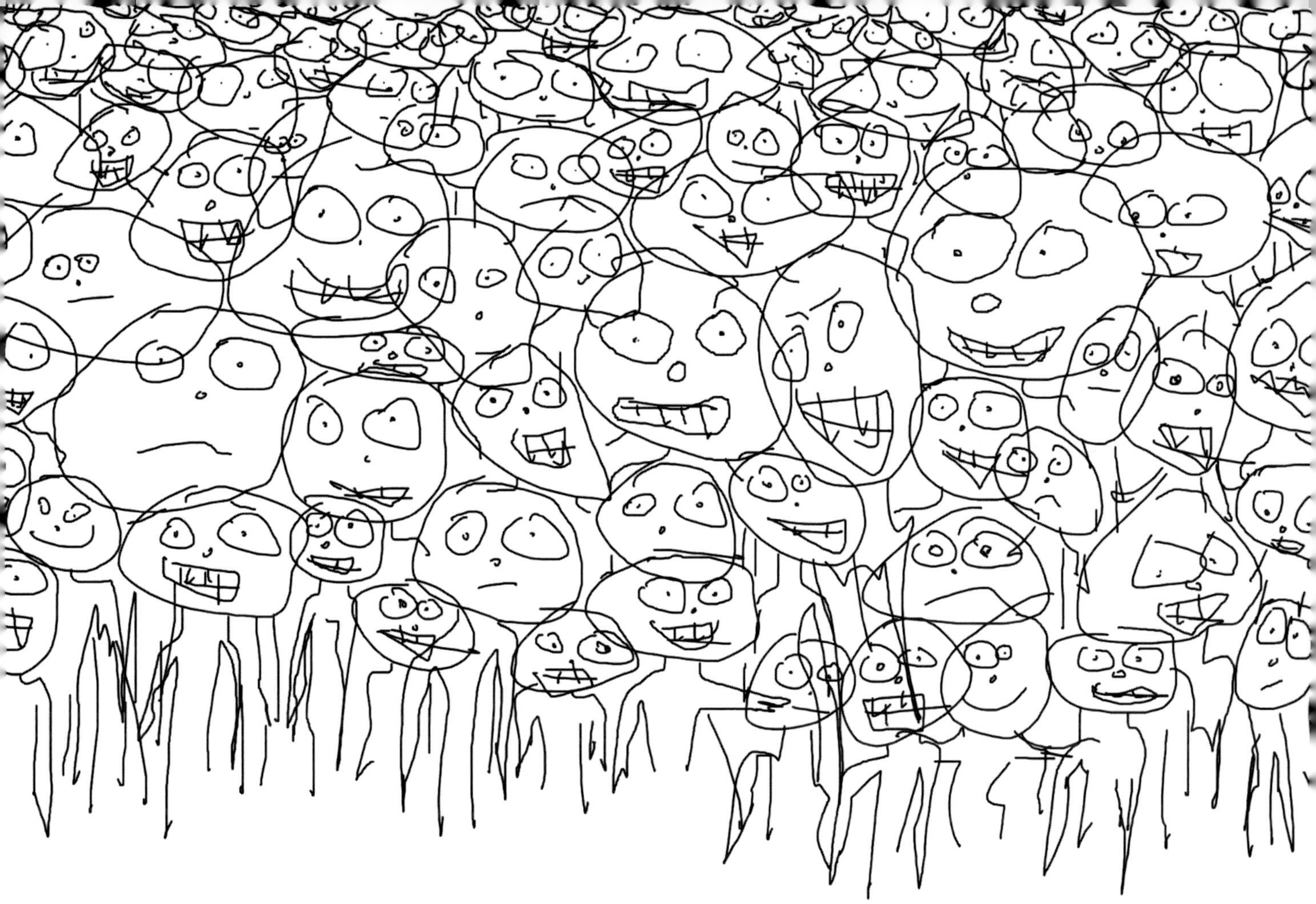

This man is confused. He has come home from drinking in the pub with his young son and remembered that it is his wife's birthday. He is drunk and has no present for his wife. His judgment is clouded by alcohol and conflicting emotions that he doesn't understand and is equally unprepared to deal with. As his boy looks lovingly up into his eyes, he realises he must return to the pub and drink more alcohol.

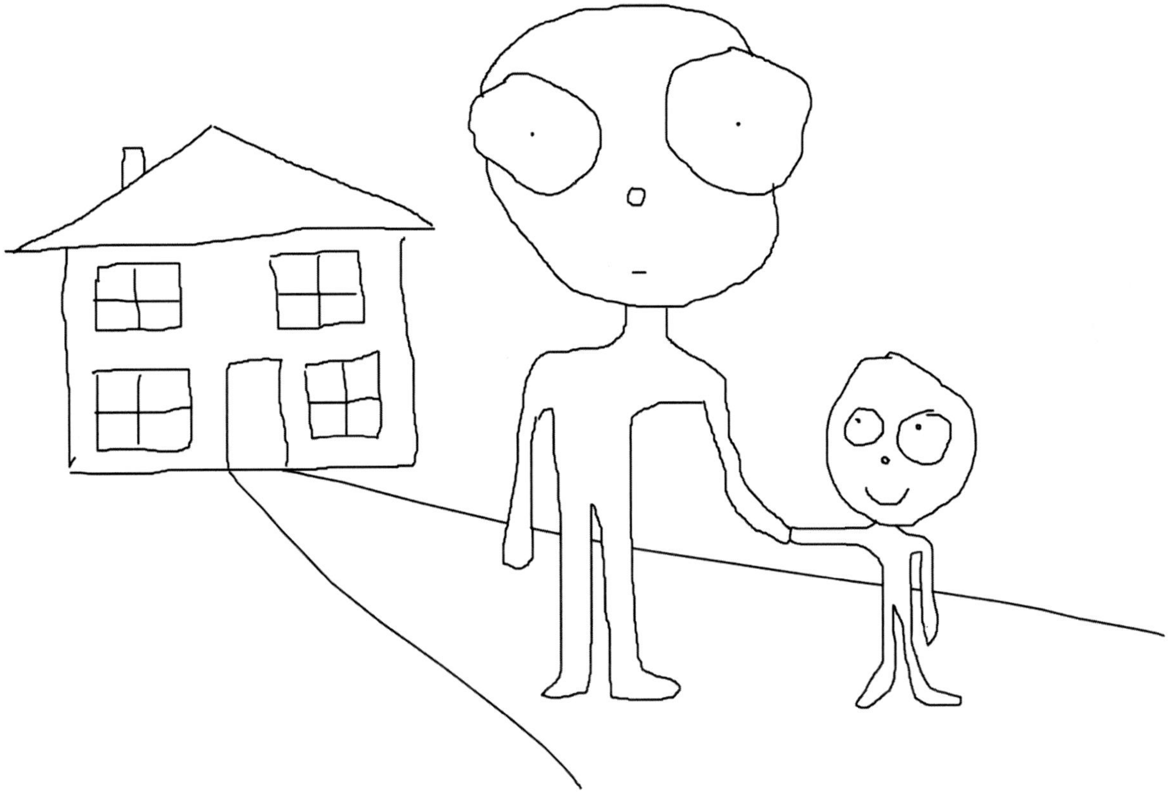

While his friends received football strips, games and money, his parents were kind enough to supply him with fresh, new textbooks. It was the best Christmas ever.

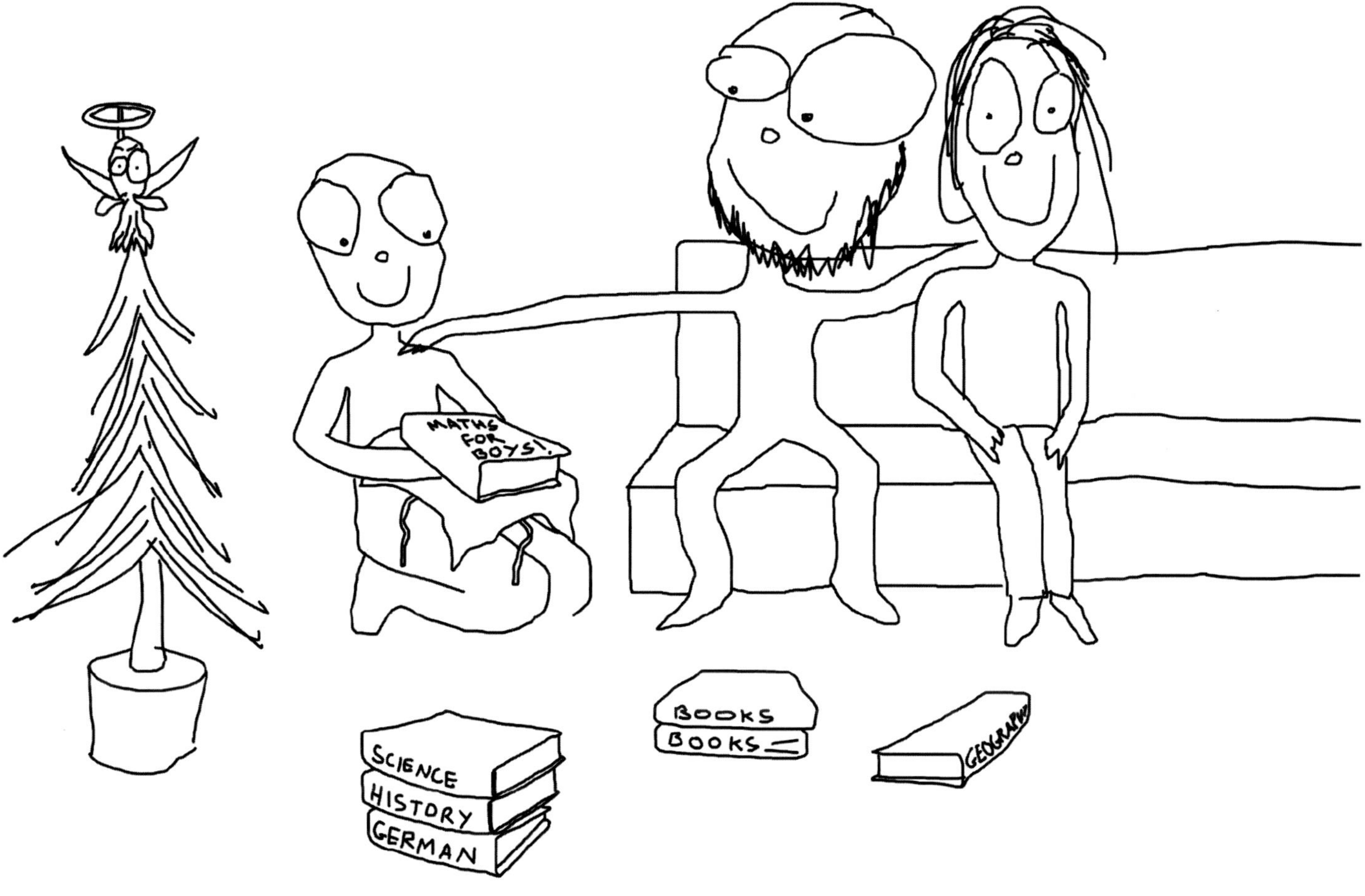

MATHS FOR BOYS!
SCIENCE
HISTORY
GERMAN
BOOKS
BOOKS
GEOGRAPHY

This is what happens to the head of a person suffering from a migraine; a big hand is trying to pop the head like a grape.

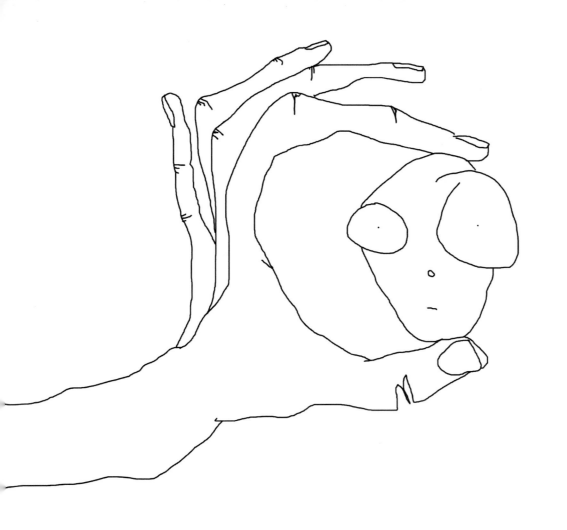

mobilophobia, *n*. The irrational fear that any conversation which is not directly mobile-phone related is both damaging to personal health and detrimental to the development of a functional and productive society.

A dog spots a thing of interest. The owner is pleased and says: "Good boy! Who's a good boy, who's the best boy, who's my best little boy, who's my best little lovely boy, who's my best little baby boo, who's mummy's bestest little baby boo boo, who's mummy's snuggely little bestest fluffy lovely baby boo boo!"

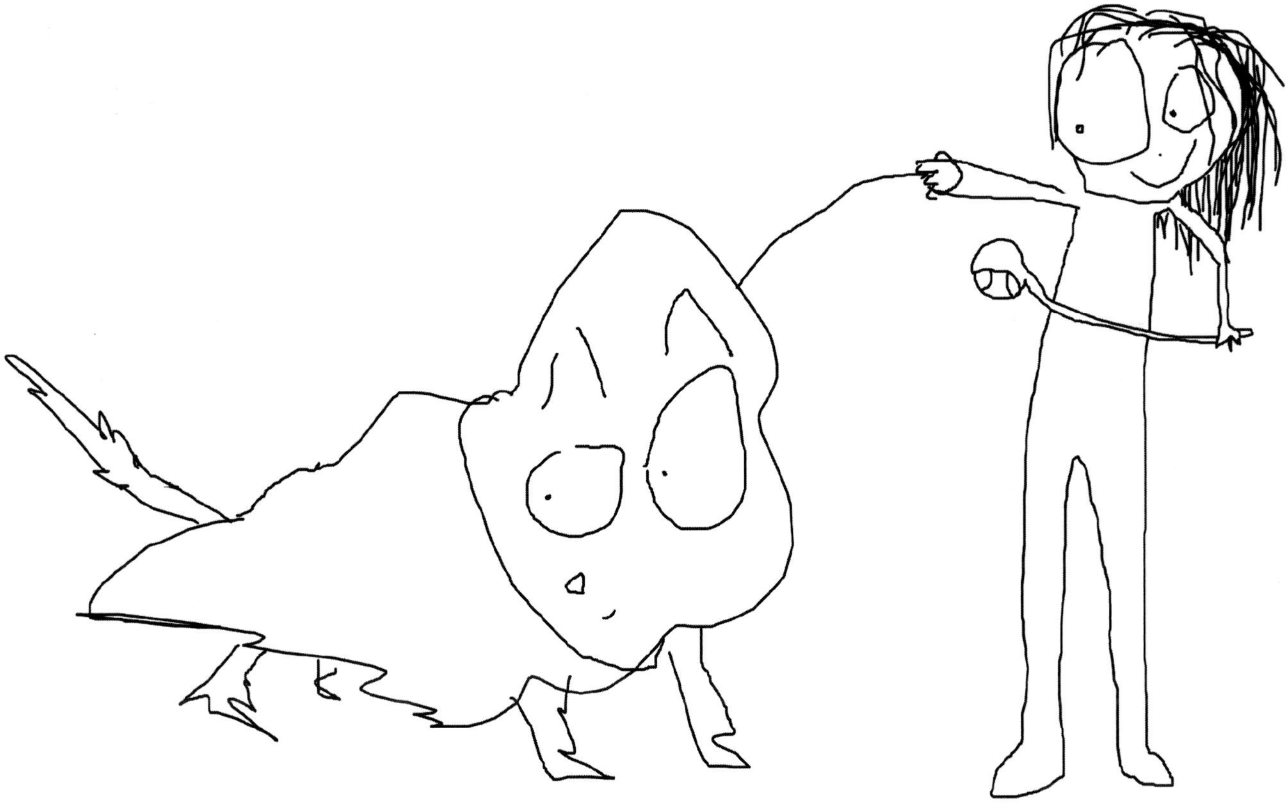

This person likes you to know that they are suffering.

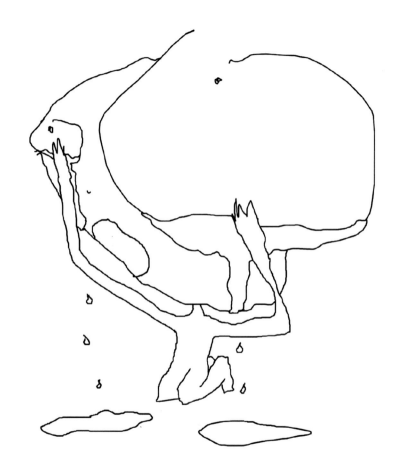

This man walks through life carrying a mask in front of his face. He is scared of people's eyes. He is scared that they will be able to see through him, thereby proving his insignificance.

Two toddlers discuss which brick to use next; it will be the most important decision of their young lives.

A group of teenage girls viciously abuse another girl because she is clever, pretty, honest, kind, generous, popular with the boys, sincere, trusting, loyal, self-deprecating, compassionate, witty, open-minded, well-read, easy-going, charming, reliable, inquisitive, musically gifted, tall, sexually active - and has nice hair.

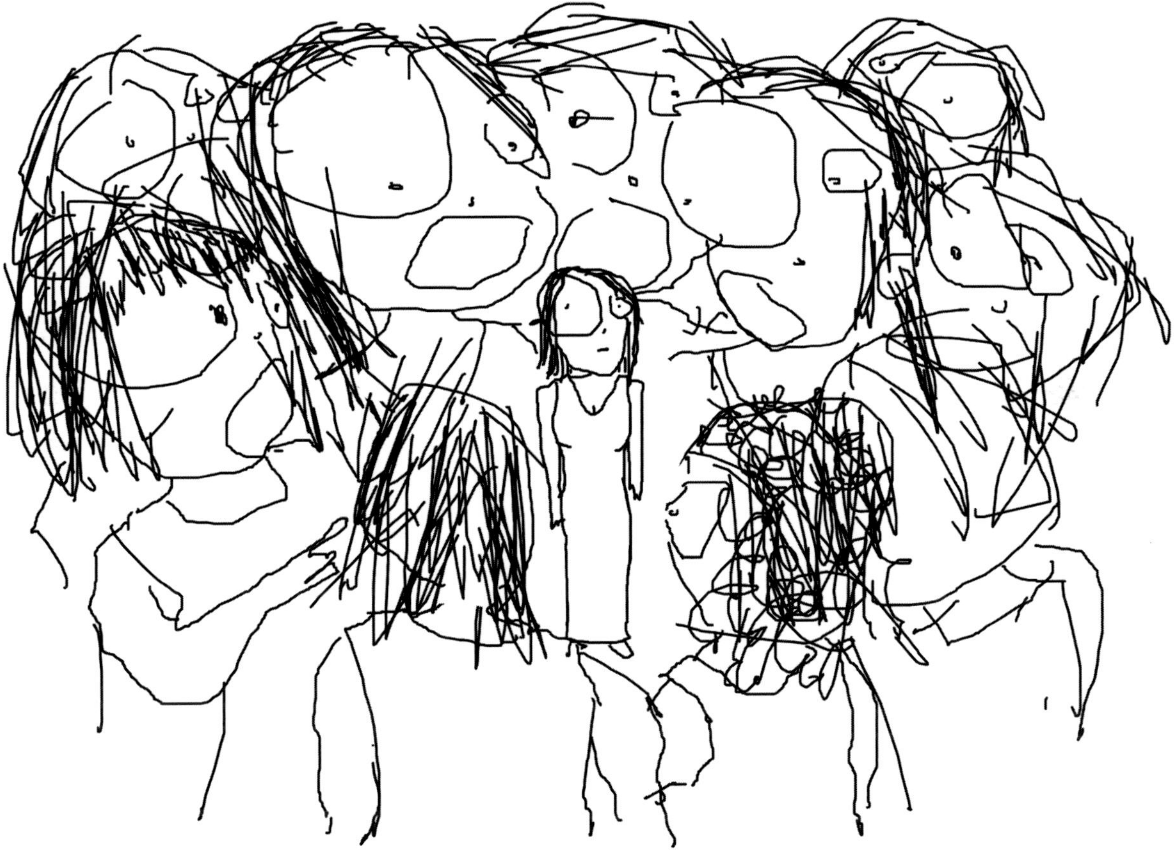

The Crazy Dancer

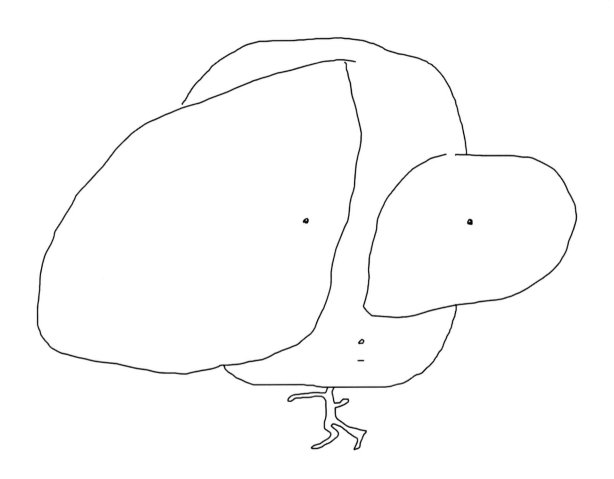

A pretty young woman is shocked by a spike on the side of a man's chin. He is equally shocked, and tries to hide his face with his right hand.

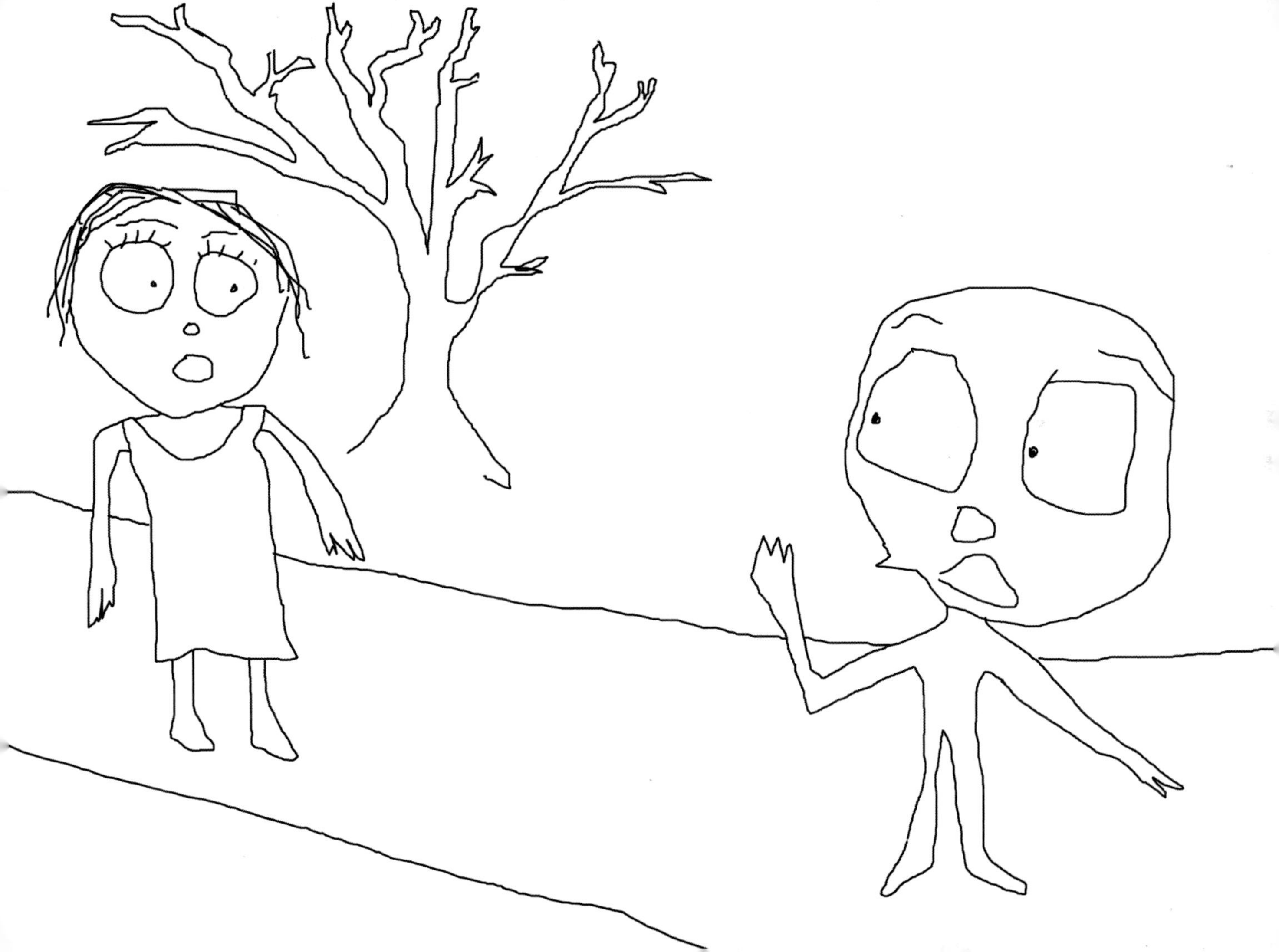

A man tries to get a perspective on his own problems, by looking at a picture of a person with no legs.

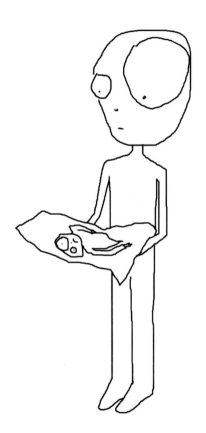

Both of these men have done 'a bad thing'. One of them made a mild *faux pas* in polite company; the other killed a man.

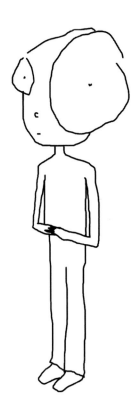

As children, two brothers started a game of hide and seek in an abandoned house. One brother was very good at hiding; the other had poor short-term memory.

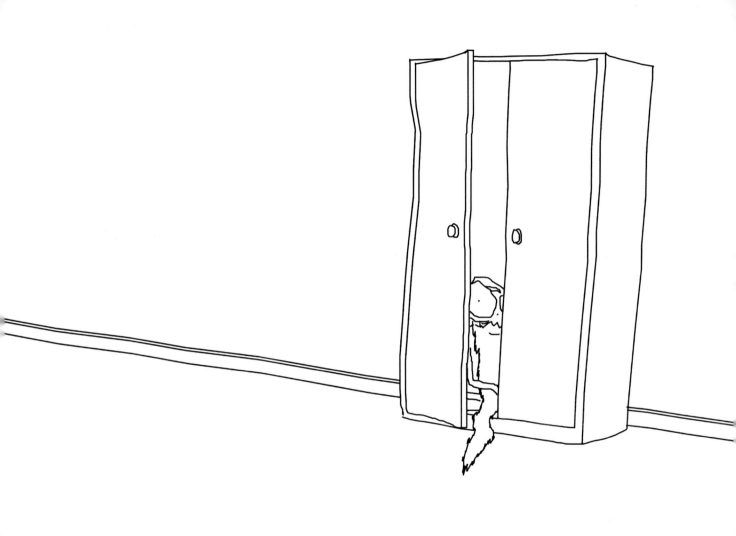

While out shopping, a young lady pauses to ponder the idea that happiness is a purely abstract concept.

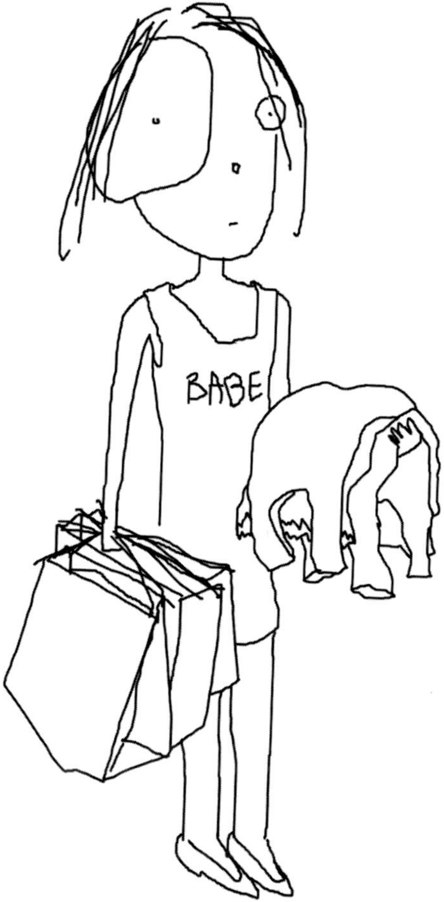
BABE

A man accidentally pulls off his best friend's head. It is only after watching the last vestiges of life drain from the eyes, that he truly understands the nature of friendship.

This man constantly looks over his shoulder in the fear that his past is catching up with him. He doesn't realise that his past can approach from the front, or either side.

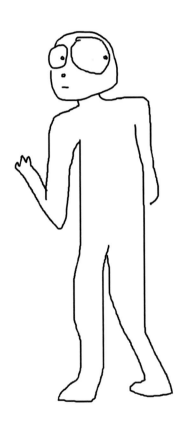

By accurately copying great works of art from previous generations, the aspiring artist is able to dispel any lingering fragments of naive inventiveness and creativity that remain from childhood.

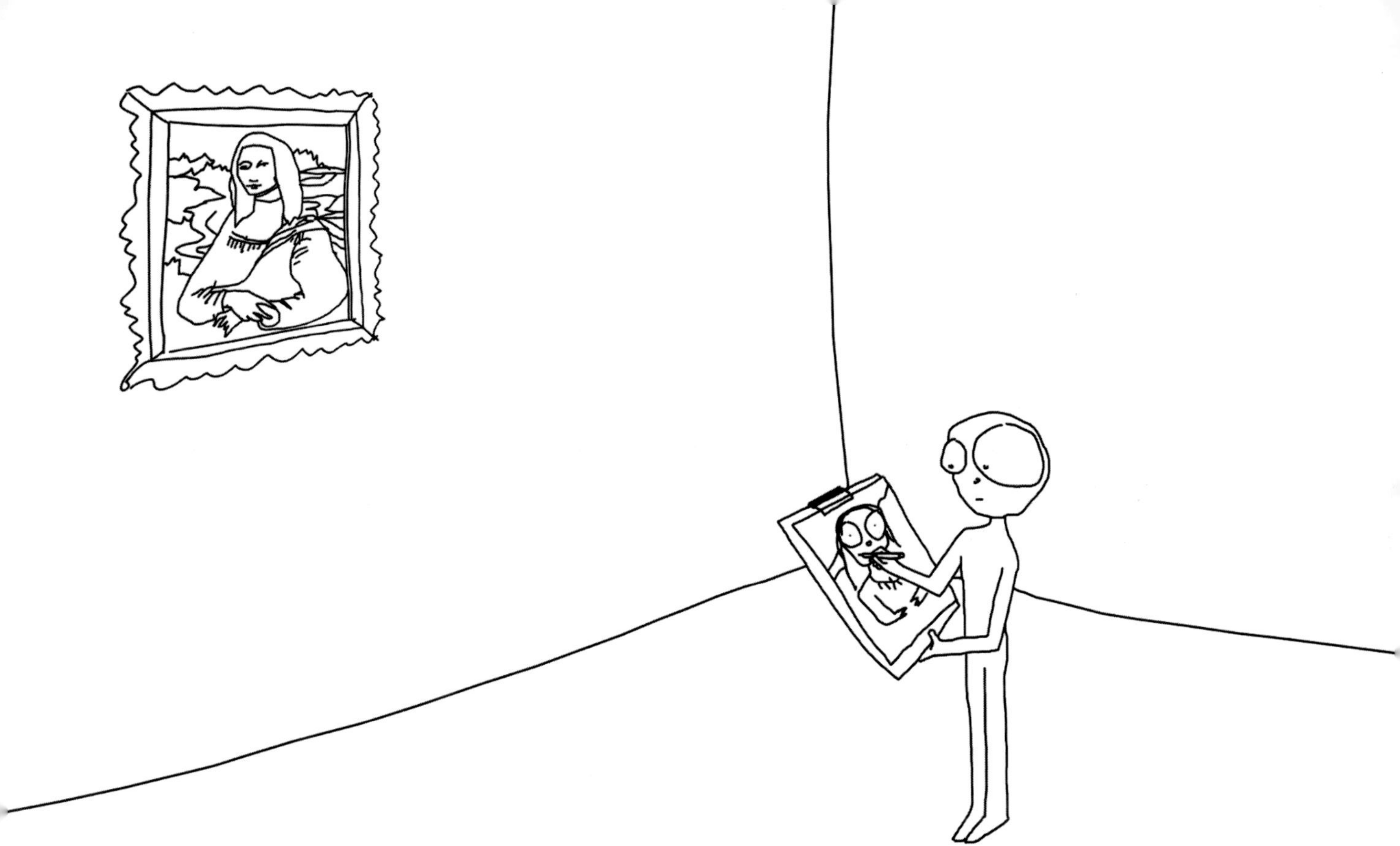

An old man stands and watches a young tree grow. At the end of his life he has found time to bear witness to nature's beauty. The gardener mows around him.

Two men: one is a manic-depressive; the other won the National Lottery five years ago.

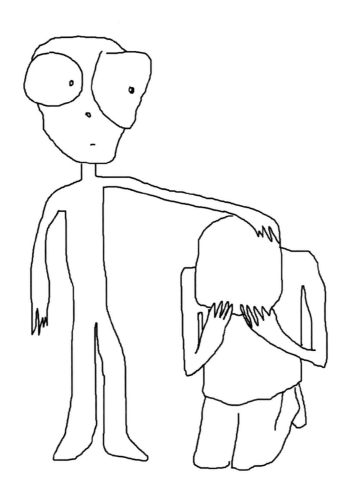

A mother is showing her son how to tie his shoelaces. She is doing her best, yet the skill she has used on her own shoes so many times before now seems to elude her.

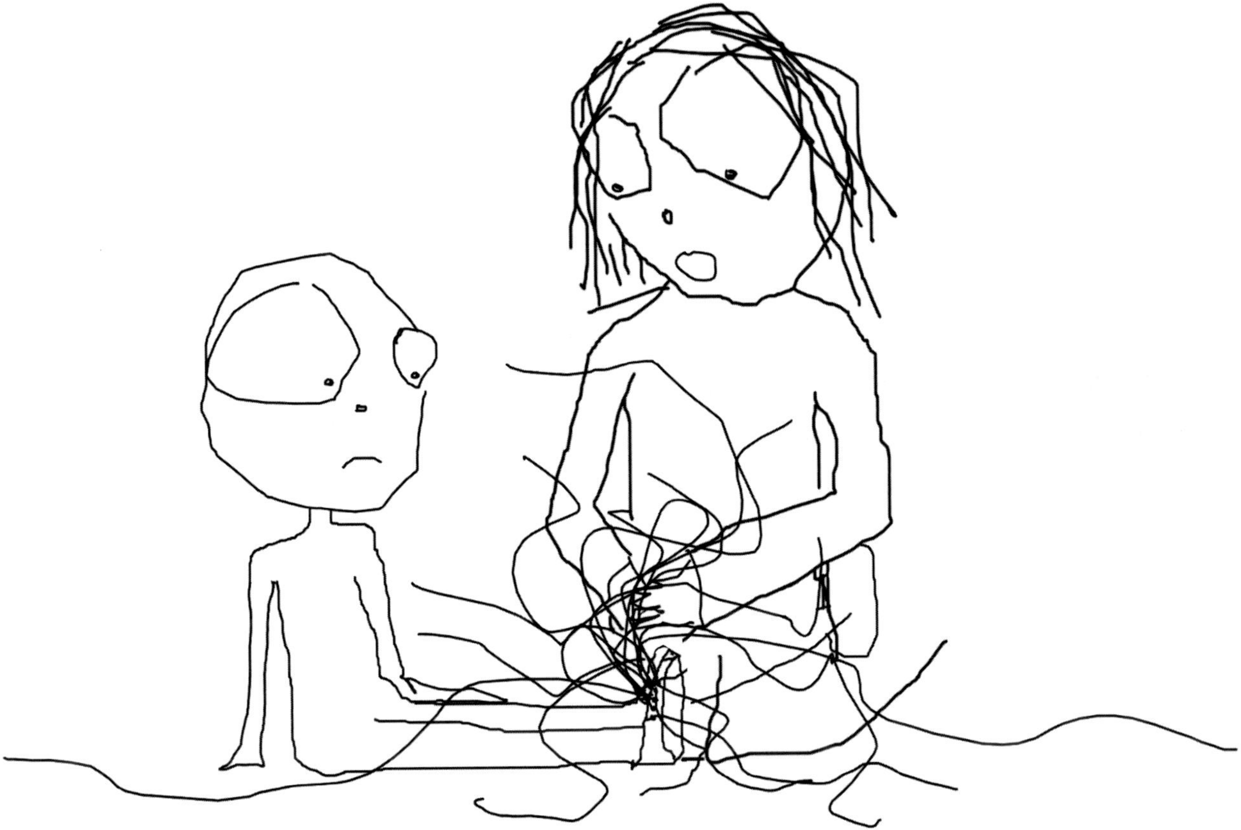

A heavily pregnant schoolboy ponders what the future holds. His child will be born into a world, not of darkness and fear, but of beauty and light.

This man lives in the perpetual fear that he will forget a close relative's birthday. He carries a pre-wrapped present with him at all times in order to protect against such events.

Within minutes of leaving the sanctuary of the father's mouth the young are completely independent, able to fend for themselves in all aspects of their lives. They are, however, still extremely vulnerable. This is mainly due to the father's predilection for eating any newborns that stay within reach. This is one of the strangest parenting behaviours in the animal kingdom and the main cause of the species' decline.

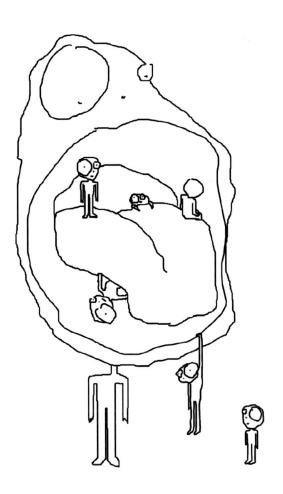

Due to his well-proportioned eyes, a man rises to the position of 'Supreme Ruler of Everything that Has Been, Is, and Ever Will Be Known'.

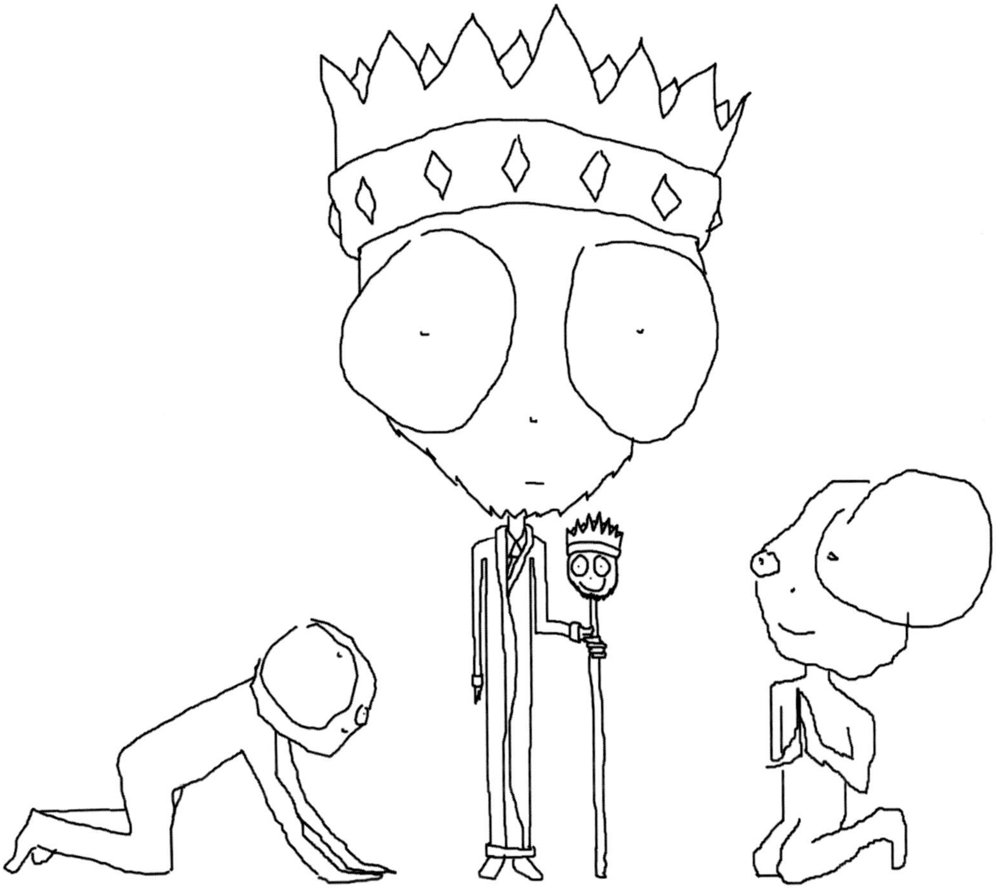

I hope you have enjoyed this book.

If you would like to find out some more about me and look at some of the other things I've done, please visit:

www.thebigeyes.co.uk

Cheers,

Simon French